"Being in love is a good thing; but not the best thing."
  -   *Clive Staples Lewis*

"Nobody has ever measured, even poets, how much a heart can hold.".
- Zelda Fitzgerald

"Love does not consist in gazing at each other, but in looking outward together in the same direction ."
- Antoine de Saint-Exupéry

"Never love anyone who treats you like you're ordinary."
- Oscar Wilde

Dedication

This collection of poems is dedicated to everyone that I have love for in my heart.
Also, to my 5th grade teacher, Diane King. She encouraged me to write, and instilled in me the power of poetry.
If it weren't for her, I never would have had the dream to become a poet and author. I know she is smiling at me from the heavens for pursueing my dream.

Blame It On My Heart

A Book of Poetry

By: Jillian A Morris

Table of Contents

A Love I Come to Repent

You are the star that guides my lonely
way
The light that fills my dark and dreary
night
The voice that soothes my sorrow and
dismay
The angel that inspires my soul's delight

But you are far away, beyond my reach
You do not know the passion that I feel
You do not hear the words that I
beseech
You do not care if my love is real

You love another, one who is not me
One who can make you happy and
content
One who can give you all that you can
see
One who can match your beauty and
your bent

And I am left to pine and to lament
To wonder what you are and where you
went
What we could of been
A love I'll come to repent

Oh, how I wish that you would look my
way
That you would see the fire in my eyes
That you would hear the things that I
would say
That you would feel the bond that never
dies

But you are blind to all that I can give
You do not sense the longing that I bear
You do not know how much I want to
live
You do not show the slightest sign of
care

You love another, one who is not me
One who can make you smile and laugh

One who can share your dreams and
fantasy
One who can be your better half

And I am left to suffer and to grieve
To hope that you will someday come to
me
What we could of been
A love I'll come to repent

But you will never know my true
devotion
You will never feel my tender kiss
You will never share my deep emotion
You will never taste my bliss

You love another, one who is not me
One who can fill your heart and soul
One who can be your destiny
One who can make you whole

And I am left to die and to forget
To curse the day that we have ever met
What we could of been
A love I'll come to repent

You Were

You were the sun that brightened up my
day
The moon that lit my lonely path at night
The song that filled my ears with sweet
array
The flower that adorned my garden
bright

But you are gone, and so went my joy
You left me in this world of grief and pain
You took away the peace that you'd
employ
You left me with a void that none can fill

You died too soon, too young, too fair,
too good
You fell a victim to a cruel fate
You left me with a broken heart and
mood
You left me with a sorrow that won't
abate

And now I wander in this dismal place
Without your smile, your touch, your
warmth, your grace
A piece of my heart that can never be
replaced
You were the sun that brightened up my
day

Her Fire Burns

A need to feel desired, a need to feel
loved,
A yearning for passion, like a hand in a
glove.
But though she longs for intimacy,
She can't see herself in his eyes

But deep within, a fire burns,
A passion that yearns, a love that
yearns.
For though she can't see her own
beauty,
She knows her heart is bright like a ruby.

Her body, a canvas, but not a work of
art,
A mirror that reflects, but not a place to
start.
For though she craves the touch of
another,
She can't see herself as a lover.

But deep within, a fire burns,
A passion that yearns, a love that
yearns.
For though she can't see her own
beauty,
She knows her heart is bright like a ruby.

The world around, a constant tease,
A reminder of what she can't be.
For though she longs to feel wanted,
She can't see herself as flaunted.

But deep within, a fire burns,
A passion that yearns, a love that
yearns.
For though she can't see her own
beauty,
She knows her heart is bright like a ruby.

So here's to the woman who longs for
love,
A heart that's pure, a soul above.
For though she can't see herself as
sexy,

She knows she's worth it, she's worth
the ecstasy.

But deep within, a fire burns,
A passion that yearns, a love that
yearns.
For though she can't see her own
beauty,
She knows her heart is bright like a ruby.

May she find the strength to love herself,
To see her beauty, to find her wealth.
For though she may not see it now,
She knows she'll find a way somehow.

Rifle and a Rack

We met out in the woods, just him and
me
He had a rifle, and I had the rack, you
see
We fell in love, under the stars above
Our bond was unbreakable, built on
trust and love

He's got the rifle, I've got the rack
Together we're a team, there's no
turning back
We'll hunt and fish, and live off the land
Our love is strong, we'll always stand
hand in hand

We've faced some tough times, but
we've never faltered
Our love is like a fire, always burning
brighter
We've been through thick and thin, and
we'll do it again

Our bond is unbreakable, until the very end

He's got the rifle, I've got the rack
Together we're a team, there's no turning back
We'll hunt and fish, and live off the land
Our love is strong, we'll always stand hand in hand

We'll face the storms, and we'll weather the rain
Our love is like a rock, it will never wane
We'll keep on moving forward, and never look back
He's got the rifle, I've got the rack

He's got the rifle, I've got the rack
Together we're a team, there's no turning back
We'll hunt and fish, and live off the land
Our love is strong, we'll always stand hand in hand

Our love is like a fire, always burning bright
He's got the rifle, and I've got the rack, tonight

Holding It In

I can not express the words on my soul
The pen won't write what's supposed to
be hidden
Revealing reality the way I see it makes
my truth real
It's best to live in the world you see me
in.
Not the world I see me in

I stay hidden from the perceived views
Locked in a fortress of fear
I've always molded to the person that fit
the person you need me to be
Being myself has never been an option

Pieces of me chipped away
Replaced by figments of your
imagination
I never grew into the person intended
Never followed a dream

Only played a supporting role in my own
life

Trying to write my own narrative
Find the person buried beneath the
blubber
No one holding my hand
No one having my back

I've crashed and burned to many times
My greatest success is always being a
failure
A burden to those chained to me by
blood
Wishing that each nights kiss would be
my last

Tired of pretending
Tired of survival
Someone grant me serenity
From the voices of my mind

Losing touch with reality
Afraid of falling behind
I must always be alright
Till the day I'm not

How much more can I hold in?

Kisses of My Life

The first kiss was a spark of light
A moment of wonder and delight
The start of a journey of love and bliss
The first kiss was a promise

The I do kiss was a seal of fate
A vow of loyalty and faith
The bond of a lifetime of joy and peace
The I do kiss was a commitment

The mistletoe kiss was a playful tease
A gesture of fun and ease
The spice of a relationship of laughter
and cheer
The mistletoe kiss was a surprise

The New Year's kiss was a celebration
A mark of hope and anticipation
The toast of a future of dreams and
goals
The New Year's kiss was a wish

The goodbye kiss was a pain in the heart
A sign of sorrow and part
The end of a story of love and loss
The goodbye kiss was a farewell

The little kisses in between were the glue of life
The moments of tenderness and strife
The essence of a connection of soul and mind
The little kisses in between were everything

They were the kisses of our life

The Heart's Way

I never think with my brain, it's too
rational and cold
I always think with my heart, it's warm
and bold
I follow my heart where it leads me in
life, it's adventurous and free
I never regret my choices, they make
me who I want to be

My heart tells me to love, to cherish and
to care
My heart tells me to dream, to aspire
and to dare
My heart tells me to laugh, to enjoy and
to share
My heart tells me to live, to explore and
to be aware

My brain tells me to doubt, to fear and to
worry
My brain tells me to plan, to calculate
and to hurry

My brain tells me to conform, to obey
and to follow
My brain tells me to survive, to cope and
to be hollow

I choose to listen to my heart, it's wise
and true
I choose to ignore my brain, it's limiting
and cruel
I choose to follow my heart, it's the best
thing I can do
I choose to be myself, it's the only way
to be happy and fulfilled

Blame It On My Heart

Some may say I'm foolish, some may
say I'm brave
Some may say I'm reckless, some may
say I'm naive
But I don't care what they say, I don't
care what they think
I only care what my heart says, I only
care what my heart feels

Blame it on my heart, it's the one who
makes me do
The things that I do, the things that I
choose
Blame it on my heart, it's the one who
makes me go
The places that I go, the places that I
know

My heart led me to love, to the one who
makes me smile
My heart led me to dream, to the one
who makes me fly

My heart led me to laugh, to the one
who makes me happy
My heart led me to live, to the one who
makes me free

Blame it on my heart, it's the one who
makes me see
The beauty that I see, the beauty that I
be
Blame it on my heart, it's the one who
makes me grow
The person that I grow, the person that I
show

My heart also led me to pain, to the one
who broke my heart
My heart also led me to tears, to the one
who made me cry
My heart also led me to fear, to the one
who made me scared
My heart also led me to loss, to the one
who made me sad

Blame it on my heart, it's the one who
makes me feel

The feelings that I feel, the feelings that are real
Blame it on my heart, it's the one who makes me learn
The lessons that I learn, the lessons that I earn

But I don't regret my heart, I don't regret my path
I don't regret my heart, I don't regret my past
I cherish my heart, I cherish my life
I cherish my heart, I cherish my light

Blame it on my heart, it's the one who makes me love
The love that I love, the love that I give
Blame it on my heart, it's the one who makes me be
The me that I be, the me that I am

The First Kiss

I never thought it would happen so soon
The moment when our lips would meet
And sparks would fly across the room
And our hearts would skip a beat

I never expected it to feel so right
The way you held me in your arms
And looked into my eyes with delight
And whispered sweet words of charm

I never imagined it would be so blissful
The sensation of your breath on my skin
And the taste of your mouth so
wonderful
And the warmth of your love within

I never dreamed it would be so magical
The first kiss that we shared that night
And how it made us feel so special
And how it filled us with delight

I never hoped it would be so lasting

The bond that we created with a kiss
And how it kept us both from drifting
And how it sealed our promise

I never wished it would be so perfect
The way you kissed me back with
passion
And how you made me feel respected
And how you showed me your affection

The Long Haul

We've been together for so long
We've seen the highs and lows
We've faced the storms and rainbows
We've shared the joys and sorrows

We know that love is not easy
It takes work and patience
It requires trust and honesty
It demands respect and kindness

We know that some days are harder
When we argue or disagree
When we hurt or disappoint each other
When we feel lonely or unhappy

But we also know that we love each
other
Even on the bad days, we don't give up
We listen and forgive each other
We support and cheer each other up

We know that the good days are great
When we laugh and have fun
When we cuddle and celebrate
When we feel grateful and blessed

We know that we are a team
We are stronger together
We share the same dream
We are partners forever

We know that this is the long haul
We are in it for the long run
We are ready for whatever may befall
We are not afraid of what's to come

Burning Flame

In the beginning, a spark ignites,
A flame that burns with all its might,
Two hearts that beat as one,
A love that's just begun.

The world is bright, the sky is blue,
The future's full of promise too,
The passion's hot, the love is true,
The world is theirs, it's bright and new.

But as the days turn into years,
The passion fades, the love disappears,
The world is dark, the sky is gray,
The future's bleak, it's far away.

The love that once burned bright and
strong,
Is now a memory, a long lost song,
The passion's gone, the love has died,
The world is cold, the sky has cried.

And so it goes, the story's told,

Of young love that was once so bold,
But in the end, it was doomed to last,
A love that's gone, a love that's past.

Finding Strength

In the beginning, love was sweet,
A heart that skipped a joyful beat,
But soon the love turned into pain,
A life that's filled with fear and strain.

The words that once were kind and true,
Are now replaced with hurtful hue,
The hands that once caressed with
care,
Now leave behind bruises and despair.

The nights are long, the days are dark,
The future's bleak, it's lost its spark,
The fear of leaving is too great,
The fear of being alone, innate.

The mind is trapped, the heart is torn,
The soul is battered, the spirit worn,
The love that once was pure and bright,
Is now a prison, a constant fight.

The world outside is full of light,
But inside, it's a constant night,
The fear of leaving is too strong,
The fear of being alone, lifelong.

But know that you are not alone,
There's help and hope, a brighter tone,
You don't deserve to live in fear,
You don't deserve to shed a tear.

There's strength in you, there's hope
and light,
There's a future that's shining bright,
You deserve a life that's filled with love,
A life that's free, like a soaring dove.

So take that step, and leave behind,
The pain, the hurt, the fear, the grind,
You deserve a life that's full of joy,
A life that's free, like a child's toy.

Waiting on the One

Although you've been divorced and
widowed,
And love has left you feeling hollowed,
I know that you still believe,
That your soulmate is waiting to receive.

It's not easy to keep the faith,
When love has left you in a wraith,
But I know that you're strong enough,
To find love again, and rise above.

The journey to find love can be long,
And sometimes it feels like everything's
wrong,
But don't give up, keep moving ahead,
Your soulmate is waiting, don't be
misled.

Love is a journey, not a destination,
And sometimes it requires patience and
dedication,

But when you find the one who's meant to be,
You'll know that love is worth the wait, and the woe.

So keep your heart open, and your spirit high,
And don't be afraid to give love another try,
For your soulmate is out there, I'm sure,
And when you find them, your heart will be pure.

Through Sickness & Health

When illness strikes,
And life seems bleak,
It's hard to find the words to speak.

But love is strong,
And love is true,
It helps us see the journey through.

We'll hold your hand,
And dry your tears,
In the depths of grief and sorrow,
I thought my heart would break,
But then I found a new tomorrow,
And love that I could make.

The pain of loss was overwhelming,
And darkness filled my soul,
But then I saw a light that's shining,
And it made me feel whole.

I thought that love had left me,
That I would be alone,
But then I found a new beginning,
And love that I had known.

It's not the same as what I had,
But it's a love that's true,
And though I miss my dear departed,
I know that I'll get through.

For love is strong and love is kind,
And it will see me through,
And though I'm still a little blind,
I know that I'll find you.

So if you're out there waiting,
And you're looking for a sign,
Just know that I am here,
And I'll love you for all time.

Finding A New Tomorrow

In the depths of grief and sorrow,
I thought my heart would break,
But then I found a new tomorrow,
And love that I could make.

The pain of loss was overwhelming,
And darkness filled my soul,
But then I saw a light that's shining,
And it made me feel whole.

I thought that love had left me,
That I would be alone,
But then I found a new beginning,
And love that I had known.

It's not the same as what I had,
But it's a love that's true,
And though I miss my dear departed,
I know that I'll get through.

For love is strong and love is kind,
And it will see me through,
And though I'm still a little blind,
I know that I'll find you.

So if you're out there waiting,
And you're looking for a sign,
Just know that I am here,
And I'll love you for all time.

Forever Bond

You and I have a bond
That is stronger than steel, that is softer
than silk
That is warmer than fire, that is cooler
than water
That is brighter than sun, that is darker
than night
That is louder than thunder, that is
quieter than whisper
That is higher than sky, that is lower
than earth
That is wider than ocean, that is
narrower than bridge

You and I have a bond
That is older than time, that is newer
than dawn
That is longer than life, that is shorter
than breath
That is bigger than space, that is smaller
than atom

That is richer than gold, that is poorer
than dust
That is sweeter than honey, that is bitter
than lemon
That is smoother than glass, that is
rougher than stone

You and I have a bond
That is deeper than soul, that is
shallower than skin
That is closer than heart, that is farther
than mind
That is clearer than crystal, that is
murkier than fog
That is calmer than lake, that is stormier
than sea
That is gentler than feather, that is
harsher than thorn
That is lighter than air, that is heavier
than rock

You and I have a bond
That nothing can break, that nothing can
bend
That nothing can shake, that nothing
can move
That nothing can fade, that nothing can
change
That nothing can hurt, that nothing can
heal
That nothing can match, that nothing
can compare
That nothing can come between, that
nothing can separate

Dear Brothers & Sisters

From deep within my heart,
There lies a love so true,
For brothers and sisters who are dear,
And whose bond grows stronger every
day anew.

We've shared so many memories,
And weathered many storms,
Our bond is strong and unbreakable,
And our love forevermore.

We've laughed and cried together,
And shared our hopes and fears,
Our bond is a treasure,
That's lasted through the years.

Through thick and thin, we've stood by
each other,
And helped each other grow,
Our bond is a testament to the power of
love,

And the strength that it can bestow.

We've learned from each other,
And grown together too,
Our bond is a shining example,
Of what love can do.

So here's to you, my dear brothers and
sisters,
My family and my friends,
May our bond continue to grow,
And our love never end.

Two Souls Collide

In the realm of hearts, a tale unfolds,
Of a love so pure, a story untold.
A journey begins, with timid steps,
As two souls collide, their hearts adept.

The world turns hazy, colors anew,
As love's enchantment takes its cue.
Butterflies dance within the chest,
A feeling so divine, it must be blessed.

Eyes meet eyes in a serendipitous
glance,
And time stands still in this cosmic
dance.
Heartbeats quicken with every touch,
As emotions soar and passions clutch.

Every word spoken feels like a song,
Melodies of love that can do no wrong.
Laughter echoes through the air,
Creating memories beyond compare.

The first kiss ignites an eternal flame,
Burning bright with an unyielding aim.
Two souls entwined in sweet embrace,
Discovering love's tender grace.

Every moment spent is filled with bliss,
A symphony of joy that cannot miss.
Whispers shared under moonlit skies,
Promises made as stars arise.

Falling in love for the first time is pure magic,
An experience so profound and ecstatic.
It opens our hearts to endless possibilities,
And fills our lives with boundless felicities.

So cherish this feeling, hold it dear and tight
For falling in love is truly a wondrous sight.

Window To The Soul

Your eyes are the window to your soul
They reveal what words cannot express
They show me the depth of your love
They make me feel blessed

Your eyes are the mirror of your heart
They reflect what you truly feel
They show me the warmth of your love
They make me feel real

Your eyes are the light of your life
They shine with joy and grace
They show me the beauty of your love
They make me feel embraced

When Eyes Meet

In a world where hearts collide,
A love story begins to unfold,
Where destiny weaves its magical tide,
Love at first sight, a tale untold.

Eyes meet across the crowded room,
And time stands still, just for a while,
A spark ignites, dispelling all gloom,
As souls connect with an enchanting smile.

In that moment, the universe aligns,
Stars dance in celestial delight,
Two hearts entwined, like ancient vines,
Love at first sight, oh what a beautiful sight!

The touch of hands sends shivers down the spine,

Electricity courses through every vein and nerve.
A connection so deep and divine,
Love's symphony plays as they both observe.

Every word spoken is poetry in motion,
Each glance filled with passion's fire.
Their souls entangled in sweet devotion,
Love at first sight, their deepest desire.

Days turn into nights without any measure
As they explore this newfound love affair.
Their hearts beat as one, bound by pure pleasure
In each other's arms they find solace rare.

For love at first sight is not just a myth
But a testament to fate's grand design.
It brings two souls together with an eternal kiss

And paints their lives with colors so fine.

So let us celebrate this wondrous delight
Of love at first sight, forevermore.
May it fill our lives with endless light
And guide us to love's sacred shore.

Waking Alone

Oh, how I long to see your face
And feel your gentle embrace
But fate has torn us far apart
And left me with a broken heart

I dream of you in every night
And hope to find you in the light
But every dawn I wake alone
And hear your voice in every moan

I write to you in every day
And pour my soul in every lay
But every letter goes astray
And every word is thrown away

I live for you in every breath
And cling to you in every death
But every moment is a woe
And every hour is a throe

Oh, how I wish to end this pain
And find your loving arms again
But fate has doomed us to this curse
And made our lives a living verse

Our Destiny

They met when they were young and
free
And felt a spark of destiny
They shared their dreams and hopes
and fears
And vowed to stay through joys and
tears

But life had other plans for them
And tore them from their fairy tale
They had to face the harsher world
And follow different paths and trails

They tried to keep in touch at first
But distance made it hard to cope
They slowly drifted far apart
And lost their faith and love and hope

They married other people then
And settled in their roles and lives
They had their kids and jobs and friends

And tried to be good husbands and wives

But deep inside they always knew
That something was not right or true
They missed the one they left behind
And longed to see them one more time

They never thought they'd meet again
But fate had one more twist in store
They crossed their paths when they were old
And felt the same as years before

They looked into each other's eyes
And knew they had to make a choice
They could not waste another chance
And listened to their inner voice

They left their old and empty lives
And ran away with their soulmate
They finally found their happiness
And proved that love is worth the wait

Soulmate

When I look into your eyes
I see the stars that light my way
When I feel your gentle touch
I melt into your embrace

When I hear your sweet voice
I hear the music of my soul
When I taste your tender kiss
I savor the flavor of your love

When I make love to you
I connect with you on every level
When I hold you in my arms
I know I have found my soulmate

We

We met when we were young and free
We felt a spark that lit our hearts
We danced and laughed and kissed and
dreamed
We vowed to never be apart

We married when we were in love
We built a home that was our own
We raised our kids and watched them
grow
We cherished every milestone

We grew old when we were happy
We saw our grandkids and their kids
We held each other's wrinkled hands
We thanked the Lord for all He did

We died when we were together
We left this world with peace and grace
We joined our souls in heaven's bliss
We found our final resting place

Center of my Life

Love is the center of my life
It fills me with joy and light
It guides me through the darkest night
It gives me strength to fight

Love is the center of my life
It makes me who I am
It shapes me with its gentle hand
It helps me understand

Love is the center of my life
It inspires me to grow
It challenges me to learn and change
It teaches me to know

Love is the center of my life
It comforts me when I'm sad
It supports me when I'm in need
It cheers me when I'm glad

Love is the center of my life
It heals me when I'm hurt
It forgives me when I make mistakes
It accepts me as I am

Love is the center of my life
It connects me with others
It respects me for my differences
It treats me like a brother

Love is the center of my life
It enriches me with grace
It blesses me with gifts and talents
It honors me with praise

Love is the center of my life
It empowers me to act
It motivates me to do good
It aligns me with my purpose

Love is the center of my life
It transcends me beyond
It lifts me to a higher plane
It draws me closer to God

Love is the center of my life
It is the reason why I live
It is the source of all that is
It is the ultimate gift

Everyday Valentine

Love is not just a feeling
It is a choice and a commitment
To care for someone every day
And make them happy in every way

Love is not just a word
It is an action and a deed
To show your partner how you feel
And make your bond stronger and real

Love is not just a gift
It is a sacrifice and a service
To put your partner's needs above your own
And make them feel valued and known

Love is not just a date
It is a lifestyle and a habit
To celebrate your partner every day
And make every day a Valentine's Day

I Fell In Love

I used to think that I was broken
That I deserved all the pain and the shame
That I was nothing but a burden
That I had no one else to blame

I used to drown myself in sorrow
In alcohol, drugs, and self-harm
I used to think there was no tomorrow
That I could never escape the harm

I used to lose everyone I loved
To violence, disease, and despair
I used to feel so alone and unloved
That I had no hope or prayer

I used to hate myself so much
That I wanted to end my life
I used to think I was out of touch
That I was not worthy of love or life

But then I met someone who changed me
Who showed me kindness and compassion
Who helped me heal and set me free
Who gave me hope and a new vision

They taught me how to love myself
To accept my flaws and my past
They taught me how to trust myself
To believe in my strengths and my path

They taught me how to love others
To forgive, to empathize, to care
They taught me how to love life
To enjoy, to explore, to dare

They taught me how to love God
To pray, to thank, to praise
They taught me how to love the world
To appreciate, to learn, to embrace

Now I know that I am not broken
That I have a purpose and a place
That I am a beautiful person

That I have grace and grace

Now I know that I am not alone
That I have friends and family
That I am a loved one
That I have joy and peace

Now I know that I am not hopeless
That I have dreams and goals
That I am a courageous one
That I have faith and soul

Now I know that I am not worthless
That I have gifts and talents
That I am a wonderful one
That I have love and life

You Are

You are my soulmate, my other half
You complete me in every way
You are my partner, my best friend
You support me every day

You are my lover, my heart's desire
You ignite me with your touch
You are my inspiration, my muse
You motivate me so much

You are my joy, my happiness
You fill me with your smile
You are my peace, my calmness
You soothe me with your style

You are my everything, my all
You mean the world to me
You are my soulmate, my love
You are my destiny

Best friend

We met when we were young and naive
We became friends and shared our dreams
We laughed and cried and fought and made up
We grew up together and learned to trust

We never thought of each other as more than friends
We dated other people and gave each other advice
We supported each other through thick and thin
We were always there for each other, no matter the price

But then something changed between us
We started to see each other in a different light

We felt a spark that we couldn't ignore
We realized that we wanted more

We were scared to ruin our friendship
We didn't know how to confess our feelings
We tried to hide our attraction and act normal
We hoped that the other one would make the first move

But then one day, we couldn't take it anymore
We decided to take a risk and be honest
We told each other how we felt and what we wanted
We kissed and hugged and smiled and cried

We were happy to find out that we felt the same
We were relieved to know that we didn't lose our friendship

We were excited to start a new chapter in our lives
We were in love with our best friend

Maybe Someday

We used to talk for hours every day
Sharing our hopes, our fears, our dreams
We used to laugh and cry and play
And make each other feel supreme

But then something changed along the way
We drifted apart, we lost our spark
We started to fight and bicker and stray
And soon we were living in the dark

Now we don't talk anymore, we don't even text
We act like strangers, we avoid each other's gaze
We don't know what to say, we don't know what comes next
We're trapped in a maze of silence and haze

But I still think of you, I still miss you so much

I still wonder what you're doing, how you're feeling, where you are
I still long for your voice, your smile, your touch
I still wish on every star

That maybe someday, somehow, we can reconnect
That maybe we can heal our wounds and mend our hearts
That maybe we can forgive and forget
And maybe we can make a new start

Forgive For Myself

You hurt me so deeply, you broke my trust
You left me in pieces, you made me feel lost
You said things you didn't mean, you did things you regret
You caused me so much pain, you made me upset

But I don't want to hate you, I don't want to hold a grudge
I don't want to live in anger, I don't want to judge
I want to forgive you, I want to let go
I want to heal my heart, I want to grow

Forgiveness is not easy, it takes time and courage
It's not a sign of weakness, it's a sign of maturity
It's not forgetting what happened, it's accepting what is

It's not condoning what you did, it's releasing what I resist

Healing is not linear, it has ups and downs
It's not a quick fix, it's a process of learning
It's not avoiding the hurt, it's facing the emotions
It's not pretending to be fine, it's being honest with myself

Forgiveness and healing are gifts I give to me
They free me from the past, they open me to the future
They restore my peace, they renew my hope
They make me whole, they make me cope

Distance

You are so far away from me
But you are always in my heart
I miss your voice, your smile, your touch
The way you make me feel

Sometimes I wonder if you miss me too
If you think of me when you see the stars
If you dream of me when you close your eyes
If you long for me when you wake up

But then I hear your voice on the phone
And I feel your love in every word
You tell me that you miss me more
That you can't wait to see me again

And I know that distance is just a test
A challenge that we can overcome
Because our love is stronger than the miles
And we will be together soon

When I Say

When you say "I Do"
You are making a vow
To love and cherish your partner
For better or worse, in sickness and health
To be faithful and loyal, honest and kind
To support and comfort, respect and trust
To share your joys and sorrows, hopes and dreams
To grow and learn, laugh and cry
To be there for each other, through thick and thin
To be a team, a family, a soulmate
To be the best version of yourself, for them and for you

When you say "I Do"
You are giving a gift
Of your heart and soul, your body and mind

Of your time and attention, your energy
and passion
Of your care and compassion, your
patience and forgiveness
Of your wisdom and humor, your
creativity and courage
Of your presence and devotion, your
gratitude and admiration
Of your friendship and partnership, your
intimacy and romance
Of your faith and hope, your love and
grace

When you say "I Do"
You are receiving a blessing
From your partner and God, from your
family and friends
From your past and present, from your
future and destiny
From your memories and experiences,
from your challenges and opportunities
From your dreams and aspirations, from
your talents and gifts
From your values and beliefs, from your
purpose and mission

From your joy and peace, from your happiness and fulfillment

When you say "I Do"
You are creating a bond
That is strong and lasting, that is deep and meaningful
That is sacred and beautiful, that is precious and priceless
That is unique and special, that is yours and theirs
That is a promise, that is a commitment
That is a journey, that is an adventure
That is a story, that is a legacy
That is a miracle, that is a wonder

A Letter of Love

In the quiet of twilight's embrace,
I stand at the crossroads of heart and
soul,
Where love's fragile threads unravel,
And destiny whispers its bittersweet tale.

The one I held, a cherished flame,
A constellation of shared dreams,
Yet life's currents pull us apart,
Tugging at the seams of our woven fate.

I release you, my love, like a paper boat,
Set adrift on the river of memories,
For sometimes love is not possession,
But the freedom to soar beyond our
grasp.

Your laughter echoes through the
corridors,
A haunting melody etched in my bones,
And I wonder if you'll remember me,
As the one who set you free, unselfishly.

The seasons change, as seasons do,
And I watch you bloom in distant gardens,
Where sunlight kisses your face,
And raindrops cleanse the wounds of yesteryears.

I let go, not in weakness, but in strength,
For love is not a cage, but wings unfurled,
And in surrender, I find solace,
Knowing that love's truest form is in release.

So fly, my dear, into the open sky,
Chase your dreams, paint constellations,
And when the night whispers secrets,
Know that my heart still carries your stardust.

And as I stand here, gazing at the horizon,

I offer you this farewell, wrapped in grace,
May life's currents carry you to shores unknown,
And may you find joy in letting go.

Living in Real Love

In the quiet chambers of your soul,
Where shadows dance and doubts take hold,
Remember this truth, etched in grace:
You are a masterpiece, God's embrace.

Look into the mirror, my dear heart,
See the galaxies within your eyes,
Each freckle, scar, and whispered dream,
A testament to love's infinite ties.

Your laughter, a symphony of stardust,
Your tears, a baptism in grace,
For you are woven from celestial threads,
A reflection of God's radiant face.

Tend to the garden of your being,
Where self-love blooms like wildflowers,
Each petal a prayer, each thorn a lesson,
Rooted in the soil of divine hours.

Embrace your flaws as sacred scars,
For they tell stories of resilience,
And when you stumble on rocky paths,
Know that grace awaits your penitence.

God's love is not a distant echo,
But a melody that sings within,
It weaves through veins, ignites your spirit,
A symphony where forgiveness begins.

When doubts whisper, "You're not enough,"
Listen to the chorus of grace,
For God's love knows no conditions,
It cradles brokenness in warm embrace.

Release the heavy armor of self-judgment,
Dance barefoot on the shores of surrender,
Let waves of love wash over your wounds,

As God whispers, "You are enough, forever."

In the cathedral of your beating heart,
Cherish the sacredness of your existence,
For loving yourself is not vanity,
But a hymn to God's boundless persistence.

Threads of love weave through time,
Connecting you to every soul that breathes,
You are not an island, but a constellation,
A part of God's cosmic masterpiece.

So love yourself fiercely, my dear friend,
For in your acceptance, you find your wings,
And as you soar on grace's gentle breeze,
Know that God's love is the song your heart sings.

Loves Evolution

In the quiet of moon-kissed nights,
Where stars conspire and hearts ignite,
I trace the contours of your soul,
As love unfurls, a story untold.

It begins with stolen glances,
In crowded rooms, fate advances,
Your laughter, a melody I crave,
A dance of fire, a tidal wave.

Our souls collide, like cosmic dust,
In whispered secrets, we entrust,
The universe weaves our threads,
 Across time's canvas, love spreads.

Your touch, electric, ignites my skin,
A symphony of senses, we begin,
Colors deepen, sounds crescendo,
In this rhapsody, our hearts echo.

Love is not armor, but naked skin,

We shed pretense, let passion in,
In vulnerability's tender grace,
We find refuge, a sacred space.

Words falter, inadequate and small,
Yet silence speaks, our hearts enthrall,
In quietude, our souls converse,
Love's lexicon, a universe.

We waltz through seasons, hand in hand,
In autumn's rustle, on sun-kissed sand,
Our bodies tango, hearts aflame,
In love's choreography, we claim.

Stars witness our covenant, our vow,
To weather storms, to cherish now,
Through tempests and celestial tides,
We navigate love's boundless rides.

But love is not immune to sorrow,
Sometimes we part, face the morrow,
Yet even in absence, love persists,
A phantom ache, a bittersweet twist.

And when eternity beckons our souls,
We'll find each other in cosmic shoals,
For love transcends earthly confines,
In stardust whispers, our love shines.

So let us write our saga, you and I,
In ink of passion, under moonlit sky,
Falling in love, a celestial descent,
Our hearts forever intertwined, content.

Eternal Vows

In the hallowed chapel's soft-lit glow,
Where time suspends and angels weep,
The groom stands, heart aflutter, breath held,
As the doors swing wide, revealing his destiny.

There she is, a vision in ivory silk,
Her gown a cascade of moonlight and dreams,
Each stitch a promise, each fold a prayer,
A tapestry woven with love's golden seams.

Her eyes, twin galaxies, seek his gaze,
And in that tender collision of souls,
He glimpses eternity—their shared infinity,
A covenant etched in stardust and whispers.

She glides toward him, a seraphic waltz,
Her steps echoing the rhythm of his heartbeat,
Veil lifted, revealing a face carved by angels,
He drinks in her beauty, a sacred sacrament.

Her smile, a sunburst after the darkest night,
Her cheeks, blushing petals kissed by dawn, H
He tastes the sweetness of forever on her lips,
And in that kiss, all past wounds are healed.

His hands tremble as he reaches for hers,
Their fingers entwined, a lifeline to eternity,
He glimpses vulnerability—the raw, unguarded truth,

And knows this love is both armor and surrender.

Her whispered vows, like petals on a breeze,
Promise to hold him through tempests and calm,
To be his shelter when life's storms rage,
And in her eyes, he finds solace, redemption.

But it's when her gaze meets his unwaveringly,
When oceans collide, and constellations weep,
He feels the weight of her "I do,"
A symphony of tears, notes written in forever.

His voice, a fragile vessel, breaks free,
"I love you," he murmurs, a confession to the heavens,
And the room holds its breath, suspended,

As love spills forth, uncontainable, unapologetic.

Time bends, stretches, then folds upon itself,
As if the universe leans in to witness,
The groom's tears, unbidden, cascade,
Each drop a baptism into love's holy font.

He weeps not for sorrow but for grace,
For the miracle of her choosing him,
For the promise of mornings and midnights,
For the eternity they've carved from fragile hours.

And so they stand, two souls at the threshold,
Bound by vows whispered and etched in stars,
He, the keeper of her heart, she, his sanctuary,
In this sacred moment, love unfurls its wings.

As the organ swells, and petals rain down,
He knows—he is seen, known, cherished,
And as they step into forever's embrace,
He surrenders to love, to her, to eternity.

Freedom of Madness

I loved you once, with all my soul and
heart
But now I see the madness in your eyes
The way you twist and tear my world
apart
With lies and threats, and cruel and cold
despise

You haunt me like a specter in the night
You fill my dreams with terror and
despair
You make me doubt my reason and my
sight
You trap me in a web of your own snare

But I have found the courage to break
free
To leave behind this hell that you have
made of me
To seek a new and brighter destiny
To heal the wounds that you have so
betrayed

And though you curse and scream and try to hold
I will not let you drag me to your fold
My life is no longer intertwined with yours
Freedom from the madness is what I behold

Dear Readers,

Love, that ethereal force that binds hearts and transcends time, defies mere words. It is the cosmic dance of souls, the symphony of vulnerability, and the brushstroke of divinity upon our mortal canvas. Love is both a whisper and a tempest, a fragile bloom and an unyielding oak. It is the language of the universe, spoken in the silent spaces between breaths.

In the sacred texts, love weaves its golden thread through the ages. The Song of Solomon sings of passion, desire, and longing—a poetic tapestry where lovers seek each other amidst vineyards and lilies. Ruth's loyalty to Naomi echoes across generations, a covenant of love that transcends blood ties. And in the New Testament, we find the pinnacle of love—the selfless sacrifice of Christ on the cross, a crimson river that redeems humanity.

1 Corinthians 13:4-7 reminds us:"Love is patient, love is kind. It does not envy, it does not boast, it is not proud. It does not dishonor others, it is not self-seeking, it is not easily angered, it keeps no record of wrong doing.It does not rejoice about injustice but rejoices whenever truth wins out. Love never gives up, never loses faith, is always hopeful, and endures through every circumstance."

My poetry is a reflection of the types of love and emotions that have shaped my world. I can only speak from my experiences, but from sharing those experiences, I hope to reach others that may feel the same way. I want to let others know they are not alone in the world and that they are surrounded by love, and they only have to look inside themselves for the best love of all.

I hope you have enjoyed my 3rd collection of poetry, and thank you for all your support and love that you all have shown me, as I bare my soul to the world through my words.

With Love,
Jillian A Morris

Epilogue

A few of the poems address mental health and domestic violence issues. If you or anyone you know needs help, please know that there are resources to help.

Mental illness affects millions of people worldwide, yet it is still stigmatized and misunderstood. It is important to raise awareness about mental health issues and to provide resources for those who are struggling. If you or someone you know is experiencing symptoms of a mental illness, it is crucial to seek help.

There are many resources available for those who need help with mental health issues. One option is to speak with a mental health professional, such as a therapist or psychiatrist. These professionals can provide counseling, medication management, and other forms of treatment to help manage symptoms.

Another option is to reach out to a support group or advocacy organization. These groups can provide a sense of community and understanding, as well as resources for finding treatment and support.

It is also important to take care of yourself and practice self-care. This can include getting enough sleep, eating a healthy diet, exercising regularly, and engaging in activities that bring you joy and relaxation.

Remember, mental illness is not a personal failure or weakness. It is a medical condition that requires treatment and support. By raising awareness and seeking help, we can break down the stigma surrounding mental health and help those who are struggling to find the resources they need to live healthy, fulfilling lives.

Mental Health Resources

1. National Suicide Prevention Lifeline: 1-800-273-TALK (8255) or https://suicidepreventionlifeline.org/

2. Crisis Text Line: Text HOME to 741741 or https://www.crisistextline.org/

3. National Alliance on Mental Illness (NAMI) Helpline: 1-800-950-NAMI (6264) or https://www.nami.org/

4. Substance Abuse and Mental Health Services Administration (SAMHSA) National Helpline: 1-800-662-HELP (4357) or https://www.samhsa.gov

5. Veterans Crisis Line: 1-800-273-8255 (press 1) or
https://www.veteranscrisisline.net/

6. The Trevor Project (LGBTQ+): 1-866-488-7386 or
https://www.thetrevorproject.org/

7. Mental Health America:
https://www.mhanational.org/

8. American Psychological Association:
https://www.apa.org/

9. Anxiety and Depression Association of America: https://adaa.org/

10. National Institute of Mental Health:
https://www.nimh.nih.gov/index.shtml

11. National Domestic Violence Hotline
1-800-799-7233 SMS: text START to
88788
https://www.thehotline.org

It's important to note that these
resources are not a substitute for
professional mental health treatment,
but they can provide support and
guidance during difficult times.

About the Author

Jillian A Morris is a talented author and poet who was born and raised in Paducah, KY. She currently resides in Cameron,TX where she runs her own wedding officiant service called The "I Do" Minister. In addition to her work as a wedding officiant, Jillian is also a wedding blogger, sharing her expertise and advice with couples who are planning their big day.

Jillian's passion for writing began at a young age, and she has been honing her craft ever since. She has published two books of poetry, including her most recent work, which showcases her unique style and creative voice. Her first book, The Composition of a Woman, received critical acclaim and established her as a rising talent in the world of poetry.

Her second book Middle Aged & Mentally ill - A Book of Poetry, is an love letter to those who suffer from mental illness and chronic health issues.

Jillian's writing is both powerful and evocative, exploring themes of love, loss, and personal growth with honesty and depth. Her work is infused with her own personal experiences, which adds a sense of authenticity and raw emotion to her poetry.

When she's not writing or officiating weddings, Jillian enjoys spending time with her family and friends, exploring the outdoors, and traveling to new places. She is also an active member of her local community, volunteering her time and resources to various charitable causes. With her talent and passion for writing, Jillian Morris is sure to continue making her mark on the literary world for years to come.

Notes: